BEFORE YOU

First published in 2012 by
The Dedalus Press
13 Moyclare Road
Baldoyle
Dublin 13
Ireland

www.dedaluspress.com
Editor: Pat Boran

ISBN 978 1 906614 48 5

Dedalus Press titles are represented in North America by
Syracuse University Press, Inc., 621 Skytop Road,
Suite 110, Syracuse, New York 13244,
and in the UK by
Central Books, 99 Wallis Road, London E9 5LN
Printed in Ireland by eprint Ltd.

Cover image 'Red bush in front of blue wall'
copyright © Glenn Nagel / iStockphoto

The Dedalus Press receives financial assistance from
The Arts Council / An Chomhairle Ealaíon

BEFORE YOU

Leeanne Quinn

DEDALUS PRESS
DUBLIN, IRELAND

ACKNOWLEDGEMENTS

Thanks are due to the editors of the following publications and websites where some of these poems, or versions of them, first appeared: *West 47, Crannóg, College Green, The SHOp, Upstart* (www.upstart.ie) and *The Stinging Fly.*

'In Paint', *West 47* online magazine, January–March 2007; 'Cockle Picker, Morecambe Bay', *Crannóg Magazine* 15, Summer 2007; 'Before You', *The SHOp, A Magazine of Poetry,* Autumn/Winter 2008 (Issue Number 28); 'Letter to Leonard Woolf' and 'Mosquitoes', *College Green Arts and Literary Journal,* 2008-2009; Excerpts from 'This is Where', 'Forebodings', and 'Rhapsody Blackout' were used in the UpStart arts collective, Irish General Election Poster Campaign, Dublin City Centre, 2011; 'This is Where', 'Poem of the Day', Upstart arts collective online blog, www.upstart.ie/blog (Wednesday April 6th, 2011); 'Rubble', *The Stinging Fly,* Winter issue 2010-2011; 'Accidents I and IV', *The Stinging Fly,* Summer issue 2011.

The author wishes to acknowledge with gratitude the assistance of The Arts Council of Ireland for a Bursary in Literature, 2010.

for Caroline Quinn

1976–1998

Contents

PART I

Imprints / 13

Mosquitoes / 14

Forebodings / 15

Graffiti on The Plant Store / 16

The Impact / 17

A House on the Ocean / 18

After Violence / 19

Letter to Leonard Woolf / 20

Gertrude Stein Poses for Man Ray / 21

Chorus / 22

Cockle Picker (Morecambe Bay) / 23

What You Will Leave Me / 24

Rhapsody Blackout / 25

Rubble / 26

Siesta / 27

Nano's Dream Castle / 28

Peculiar Alphabets / 29

Eating Out / 30

Permafrost / 31

In Paint / 32

Berlin / 34

Ode to Memory / 35

Giving Rain / 36

The New Heart / 38

After / 39

Absence of Memory / 40
This is Where / 41
Frequent as the Naked Dream / 43
Winter Coat / 44
Naples / 45
Acoma / 46
Before You / 47

PART II

Storms / 51
Houses / 55
Water / 59
Accidents / 60

⌒

NOTES / 64

The islands haven't shifted since last summer,
even if I like to pretend they have
—drifting, in a dreamy sort of way,
a little north, a little south or sidewise,
and that they're free within the blue frontiers of bay.

—Elizabeth Bishop, 'North Haven'

I

Imprints

When I burn my hand
and don't cool the skin
under cold water
until the cold aches
but not the burn
I hear your voice saying
I'll never get the sting
from it like that time you hit me
on the beach in Brittany
when too young to care
about scenes we broke into one
of our furious brawls
you stunned me
with the smack of the spade
on skin already sun-burning
among soft accents
you ran for cover
quick as a rock-lizard
leaping jellyfish
that lurked like landmines
on the taut wet sand

Mosquitoes

We were travelling into the dust-roads
and white sands of our imagination.
We were spinning maps on the axis of your globe,
picking places big enough to hold us both
together. Geography was soil and rock until we landed
with two fingers upon the cartographic shape
I knew in name only.

Little did we know how the sun would burn
every last cord between us, leaving us battling
through insect-thick nights for a bigger patch
of the sibling world. As you basked in our independence
I hid from a sea that smarted every part
of my home-sickened body
as if I were the rocks that contained it.

As I counted down days of magnetic sun
you swam in from your rage
and casually, as if requesting the time, asked me,
Do you think I am a good person?
I answered honestly but you took it as truth
and swam back to a sea—a cerulean blue
I have never known.

Forebodings

The seagulls are in from the shore again,
airborne scavengers, sounding their foreboding—
over grey, capital skies they float, wise enough.
It has rained everyday for two months,
a layer of mud swells like a quenched tongue
beneath grass too wet to cut. On the screen

Glastonbury is another washout
of wellingtons and ale, while a heat wave burns
through southern Europe. Greece is on fire,
gorse-lit and arid. A man takes shelter
under a wide-brimmed hat and explains
the extent of the damage—house, farm, land,

all went up, burned like paper, but for longer.
I leave him standing in heat almost audible,
while outside heavy clouds hover
over rooftops. The seagulls have retreated.
A car alarm sounds in their place as the rain breaks,
like a splay of bullets, from the bloated sky.

Graffiti on The Plant Store

The words are perfectly formed,
silver and bold, they cut through the centre
of the boarded-up store. Words well-worn,
yet here, this morning, I can see people
glancing sideways, reading their simple
proclamation, wondering if they are
the *you* who is *beautiful.* A woman
carrying a tray of coffee like a bomb,
slows down as she passes, and watching her
readjust to the possibility,
I wonder who, in some in-between hour,
came out here to disarm us.

The Impact

It is late evening when the shouts
of local boys and girls begin. Across this city
street they shoot footballs, bottle tops,
hot chips from the chip shop whose steadfast
neon light shines opposite my window,
more dependable than summer sun.
Car horns bleat intermittantly, or tyres break
to a dead halt, and each time I look out
I expect to see some body flung
far from itself, broken to a new form—
but the cars only ever move on, trailing
coarse words that illicit appreciative roars.
As evening darkens and turns the windows
of vacant houses black, they gather under
the light of a lamppost, blow cigarette smoke
in fat rings that grow thin, imperfect halos.
As the smoke reaches a bouquet of flowers
tied above them on the lamppost,
I wonder if they know what misfortune
it marks—though wilting now, I often wake
to see them blooming. As they begin
to move on, a small boy flicks
the butt of his cigarette at the windscreen
of an oncoming car, his parting gesture.
For a moment the embers flare
magnificently, a cheer goes up
in recognition of the boy, his daring,
the unexpected beauty of the impact.

A House in the Ocean

Half-submerged, a house floats
on the ocean. Its roof and second story
protrude from the surface—a curious island

of brick and glass, supported now
by the unsteady sea—the wreck
of its contents scattered

where a lawn could be, shook
and shot about like an abandoned
building lot. Will the sea

bear its inhabitants home?
Or do they already lie adrift
on pummeled land, inconsolable

as this rootless house,
still looking like it could keep
the outside out.

After Violence

Before us there is only horizon,
the clean line signalling the apparent
meeting of earth and sky. Where we are

is of little consequence when, at this speed,
a sudden impact could reduce us both
to steel and glass and taint the air

with that unnatural hue that settles
after violence. The words you pitched
against gravel become smoke

in your throat and spent oil burning
the only sound. But just before we break
away from the world, I am almost certain

you say something about distance—
how it is the heart's limitation.

Letter to Leonard Woolf

I walk outside, leaving the house behind.
I want to go quickly, to the city—
to London where there are voices

other than my own. I hear too little here,
I'm stuck like the moth pressed to the glass,
teased by the light behind this thickening

air. This countryside has its moments
for being but I am not myself.
I cannot write—the deadening heat

dulls me. I must leave. We have known this
ending. I am cruel, careless with your fear,
driven by my own impatience with this

thin veil of life. I wait as the current resounds
in me, whirring like the engine of the world.

Gertrude Stein Poses for Man Ray

with one eye on an opened door. Poses
and sits in opposition to the lens,

knows the right angle for genius
is darkness. Framed against shadow,

the damp future, the Picassos hanging ripe
for repossession, one quick thought

escapes the camera's detection, as Ray, poised
for greater things, scurries up figures, knows

money oils the mind. Here, where genius sits
like a noun in limitation, where one name

makes a phantom of another, and no one
outlasts their creation.

Chorus

Consonants knocked
together like blocks

of frozen sea, or
the plates of continents

moving, a dangerous time to be
near you, and all ears.

Cockle Picker (Morecambe Bay)

You watched the rain bury itself deep
into the bed of the ocean. The sea
rose and dipped, butterfly waves,
unsettling the working day, masking
the creeping tide. You went out into the shallow
water—sought the heart-shaped shells, lifted
them as if catching currency and not
the sea itself. You made the familiar
line, a bearing in a chain, your outline cast
against the blackness of the waves. But the sea
deceived, took back its wares, and cut you off
like a door slammed tight and bolted.
You fell in with the tide, became scattered
in your salt-stricken panic, struggled from
your clothes, clung to nothing, felt the swell
of suffocation, the blood explosion—
bursting, gave yourself up, naked, poorer—
your body brimming, full as the sea.

What You Will Leave Me

You place the figure in the centre
of the floor—a girl with wrought arms
reaching upwards—and tell me this

is what you will leave me.
You talk of light and space, and move
as if you could generate both,

though the room stripped bare
couldn't hold her bronze proportions
or keep her stillness from being

anything other than a reminder
of this moment, of this room,
of the two hours you have travelled

with her, bubble-wrapped and secured,
sure that I will love
what you love. Sure that I will see

in her poise a familiar past—
a delicate restitution for the future.

Rhapsody Blackout

Darkness bodies us without
shadow, the opaque moon
brings no light here
as we seek to repeat love,
echoing what has come before.
Outside, where dogs return
each other's bark, the night
calls itself full, becomes old
night, unblemished by the sun's
scarring presence. Now nothing
can be seen that is not felt—
here where our bodies
are once again enough,
featureless as silhouettes,
known only by the need
that leaves us feeble-eyed,
gaping outward into black.

Rubble

Take this house from my body, brick from my bones. There's my foot under yours. Take it. It will make you rich. Wrap me in your heroic sheet. Cover your face, I'm decomposed. Carry me out. See how I fit inside, how my spine curves to these dirty threads. Oh you can hardly make me out. Oh make me out. Prose me, poem me. Put flesh on these blanketed bones. Bundled, compare me to the stork's gift. Oh call me rubble, the earth has done worse. Loot me, lyric me. Pick at my bones.

Siesta

When this place sleeps it sleeps without you,
nurturing a body you cannot see.
Long into the afternoon, the quiet marks you

as a stranger. These streets, brick-red
and worn, tell you you must earn your healing,
as though reprieve is not for you. Here, the sun

needs something to burn itself into. Today
it is you and your tired skin knows
there is no shade cool enough to calm

these hours when you live as though it is
your shadow that has cast you, narrowing
itself like the eye of a needle, to the point

where the day leaves you unsung and moored.

Nano's Dream Castle

I surface where the dream begins, oiled
in autumn you've made me visible,

lifted me out from under my muddy
hues. Trees weave shape to my canvas,

your russet night brighter than my light-
denuded day. You've given me a face

that rivals your yellow moon—
incandescent it circles my castle.

Painting the painter, lurking
knee-deep in primitive reeds,

you've made a chameleon
of my mind, and called it my own.

Peculiar Alphabets

Love made us a language we were incapable
of using. We could not recognise our words
or discover meaning in their strange

intonation. We threw them out, carelessly
bandied them about like Sunday mornings.
But I could not read the suggestions

colouring your eyes or know the patterns
of their changing. The way your shoulders moved
when you spoke, the way my fingers tapped

the beat of our talk on an unsteady table,
told us nothing. No, for days—or maybe
years—we lay safe and earthed, wrapped

in our soil-skins, waiting for the dig to begin.

Eating Out

Consumed by a couple who sit in silence,
you interrupt me just to point out how

this particular pair eat without speaking.
She, head downcast, attends to the task

of picking white fish from its springy bone.
He stabs at his food as if puncturing

the air between them. While you,
dissatisfied, almost hurt yourself

looking past me for explanations.
There's something wrong here, you say,

not to me but to the scene unfolding
mutely behind me, as if you should get up

and fix it. As if their not-talking
is something they have forgotten,

something they have left behind,
so you can call after them—

half-embarrassed by your heroism—
and disrupt their do-not-disturb

alliance, while I sit appetite-less
reading the menu, like a page-turner.

Permafrost

Darkness brings us full sphere and becomes
a sleeping kiss. A warm softness to it,

the remnants of a bitter winter when
the violent baring of colour becomes

the season's refrain, and dead wood burns
in place of candles in the open-mouthed

fire. Where does time for us begin amidst
the strictures of change... Are domestic fires

the height of things? Or should we burn
the seasons into a cacophony of flames,

until the leaf-drenched lanes become
brittle and crack under the pressure

of our resistance... Like this, we bring
another year across an invisible line,

and readjust once more to save ourselves
from the black permafrost.

In Paint

Against pain I steady the canvas,
a mountainous metal space,

with oil keys I enter. Defiant,
I go to the glass. A flower burnt

in a Mexican sun, I watch, no,
observe my stillness. I do not see

beyond skin while taking measurements
with my fingertips—

unsympathetic receptors.
The first touch of paint sets the tone—

restrained, meticulous, no gorging
on the unconscious here.

Despite what they say I am a realist,
depicting only my experience,

daily lived in magenta, sorrowful
green, maddening yellow. Fictions

to accompany the fictions—
despite what I say. I drink

from a murky glass, swirl tea,
at times tequila, cut my own hair,

think I am more beautiful
than the women I share

my husband with as if he were
a vast piece of fruit, quartered

and passed around a thirsty room.
I perform loneliness well

but am in fact happier alone
with only my dog to kick out

from under me, away from the paint
and the brushes abandoned like words

waiting to be finished. In this room
I am the only speaker. Again

and again I dress myself
in paint. My hands knuckled

like a knotted rope seduce me
to my own end and persuasion

is not needed. Like a moon
beginning, I unveil myself

with a half-smile. In a fading
monthly light, metal becomes mirror.

Berlin

Without the maps of our known lives we feel
our way through others' histories, seeing
neither past nor present. As we move

among our imaginings of how people
here live, glimpse in half-opened, heavy
doorways the beginnings of a life,

I can't cast off the feeling that we are
marring this city for each other. Etching
ourselves onto its already pared walls,

leaving togetherness in everything
we touch, so that we stay framed
in subterranean windows, wearing this city

as a scar we cannot yet see, nor heal.

Ode to Memory

I

The sea is blue, the air above the sea is sea-
coloured. We stare at the horizon, the apparent
meeting of earth and sky. A couple argue on the rocks
below. Their words reach us, wind-warped.

II

The sea is blue-coloured, the air above the sea
reaches the horizon. A couple argue.
The rocks below mark the apparent meeting.
The wind warps words, earth, and sky.

III

There is no sea, the air is night-coloured.
We argue on the rocks, our words
reach the horizon. Earth and sky
mark the apparent, below.

Giving Rain

We hid from the rain
under the husk of a tree. Its roof of leaves
covered us for as long
as they could withstand the sky.
As the soil began to absorb us,
to drink from our clothes as if they were life-

giving, you said life
here could be as before. While the rain
rising, kept us
standing under wet leaves
that betrayed no one, the sky
became undone, long

past blue, long
past "before". What life
did you imagine living with your sky-
grey face turned from the rain?
A life where no one leaves
one love for another? As if keeping us

here could keep us
from ourselves, but the long
day leaves
us with only our life.
It will rain
until we stop resisting, until the sky

empties itself of sky,
and sees us
stepping into a road that rain
has made river-like. We sheltered for too long,

looking like stilled-life,
as wet as the leaves

that know only how to be leaves,
unconcerned with outwitting the sky.
We lived as though our life
could be washed from us,
seeped through us, long
after the rain

unravelled us, long after the leaves
had dried and the sky
relented, giving rain, giving life.

The New Heart

I

The new heart beats a
path to our old door shut tight,
cul-de-sac of love.

II

The new heart speaks out,
until its low, rough rhythm
silences your name.

III

The new heart unfurls,
unmasks memory, breaks
our fickle cord of love.

After

Death was the drowned body of a boy
you'd kissed. Excelling seaward,

a riptide exhausting his life, nothing
could undo the hot day's damage,

though you sat repeating his name
as if it might. From then on

rivers were fatal, riptides eerily real.
I thought of that day after you died,

when summer had shown us
just what was possible. A boy was gone

and you grieved. I remember
your face in the too bright light

understanding nothing,
yet full of knowing.

Absence of Memory

At the end of each day I dispel
into meaning the absence and presence
of you, and think how I have tied myself

too vigorously to the habit
of half-truths and home-spun sentiments.
I should, instead, comb the world for facts

of you, put them into clear jars—marked
by date, and time, even. Then I would
dispatch them into the stratosphere

of hereafters, and wait for a light to blaze
across this thin-skinned sky, as proof
that there is still something of you

that cannot be reached by memory.

This is Where

You phone from another country,
I can't remember where or why
you're calling. I can't hear
what you're saying
until I soon realise
you're explaining yourself
or more specifically
your absence. Then my room
becomes another, familiar
yet far from where I should be.
A noise keeps coming,
a noise that makes me tense
my shoulders as if something
is about to fall on either
one of us. You crackle
on the other end of the line,
your voice changing into one
that isn't yours. And then
your body goes too, from
right before me, subdued
by the din that is all
of a sudden everywhere.
What city are you in,
I hear myself saying.
I almost know, I almost feel
the answer rise to my lips,
the word that will fix what
is broken here. I can't make
my mind reach it. I say your name
instead and suddenly

you're gone, quick as a
guillotine the line goes dead,
and the silence rings in my ear
like a punishment.

Frequent as the Naked Dream

Frequent as the naked dream where I
descend into unconcealed panic,
no clothes on a peopled street, faces
full of knowing, you appear. And anything
can happen here. Sometimes we talk,
conversations we've never had,
embraces that feel unsaid. But mostly
we argue ourselves into duplicate rage
until I wake, bundled like strewn clothes,
awaiting the return of my body,
in a world where you are not
and where I never forget to dress.

Winter Coat

Your winter coat hangs inside my wardrobe.
An object memory I cannot trust.
Though it hasn't kept your body warm

in years, been trudged through rain or wrapped
by wind—the kind that animates dead leaves—
it retains your shape, like the cindered frame

of a fire log. Past meaning, it is out
of season, and holds nothing
I can touch, except this strand of hair

woven to the collar, a remainder that marks
only absence, as it glistens still
on this coat that is no longer coat.

Naples

We took pictures in the Piazza
Garibaldi, three of us then,
pressed together and newly framed

by what we knew about the present.
We walked to the sea. The bay,
arched and blue, revealed itself

like a trick of the mind, mirroring
our week-old selves. Looking back
to Capri, to its rubbled sand,

to Vesuvius, calm and sated,
I thought this is the distance
we have travelled without you.

This is the earth's irreproachable
response to your absence.

Acoma

Furtively, like the moon receding,
light consumes the room. My own sky
city, trapping heat, warming

the amber walls, lessening the cold
echo of an empty house.
There is movement, still that

familiar sound of doors knocking
against nothing. People passing,
frequent and blameless as before.

Wrapped in particles of winter
light, I put away these days
as if closing a cupboard door

or tightening a parched tap
could set the sun.

Before You

It was all crimson or black anyway,
eyes opened or closed it looked good
out there, when things were still

beyond reach and no one had come
to warn you of your potential
like you were wood or stone, waiting

to be something made from wood or stone.
And the sun didn't need to be fixed
to a certain height or lowered

to a specific point, for you to be happy.
It was glamorous too, in the pre-emptive
stage, when you had gathered yourself

to yourself as if you were love or
simply something warmer
than your own skin. The air

was breathable then, it took from you
and was returned
unblemished. And with that, life

was in the wings, beating a silent drum
before you, telling you this,
and this, and this.

II

Storms

I

What were you thinking when the roof blew off your solitary room. Had the storm come to this, sinister, had it found you wanting. Trespasser, walking in the bat-filled woods, gathering ground. And in the forest you heard owls and dreamt at night of owls, of an eyeless, owl-less man. What were your dreams telling you. That the bats will follow you home. That the owl's malevolent hooting is made for you alone, just as the road that winds its way up to a mountaintop house is mapped to the outline of your life. Though you don't yet know it, it will lead there and return you.

II

How cold it gets when there is no warmth to direct you. The seasons are inverted, clouds sit upon your window and blight your chest; asthmatic wheeze past midnight. What time does midnight occur here. How long after the lights go out do you re-emerge, working your fingers to the flame-empty oil-lamp. Who watches through the window and remembers nothing in the morning.

III

Your father died when he was thirty-nine. Do you remember
when the hurricane shook the windows until you were sure
they would shatter inwards. What was the noise that kept
coming back. The sound of the shutter was like a hand
slapping your face. You were consistently surprised by your
hand holding the side of your face. Rain scarred the window;
your forehead beaded sweat. The house, exhausted by the
effort, fell silent near morning.

IV

Lightening hit the mountain, relieving the night of itself. You woke while the floors seemed to be moving. The sound was scurrying, catching itself. You were not in any place that you knew. The sound did not know you. Then you saw the electric blue of the Toucan's feathers. And you knew why you remained. The sound brought you back to sleep and the floor steadied itself for morning.

Houses

I

Bare walls made bad companions. The windows made promises they couldn't keep, though you reached for them and bore cold weather well. Barefoot, sometimes in winter. And in the village you were stranger; not understanding the unspoken. Even now the soundlessness of morning creeps its way to your ear.

II

When you left you took everything with you. Spent your time opening and closing doors until you were the time that elapsed between the opened and closed door. Always comparing the walls to what you had seen before; the streets to where you had walked. There was comfort though, and much more. You rearranged what you could to fit yourself inside, like one body fitting itself to another's. Warmer, though the sound of snow still lingered.

III

You built walls around a scream but it grew louder until the southern heat muffled it. The past was still an open mouth. The body you reached for at night could not close it. The skin was damp under your hand. It had nothing to do with the weather.

IV

From your window you could see water. The air tasted of salt and your skin browned. You knew how to name the things you saw and in what order they should be named. You waved to yourself from a height but you were looking the other way when you waved back.

Water

memory followed you
on the water and grew
roots
in the sun   your body
broke
the surface and the day
was new   water
turned to sea
a blue too blue
even when night darkened it
you could still tell
its colour the way closing your eyes
makes nothing disappear

one sea became another
tankers dragged themselves
over the bay   slow
sluggish bodies
tired of the habit
of inhabiting
themselves   of feeling
the weight
of what they carried

Accidents

I

The year revolves again, habitual
as a ring inscribed and turned round
your finger. Circular and forward

as the face of a clock, dumb to repetition,
its own Sisyphean rock. January brings
in the old feeling, anchors the blood,

which is all the body can renew—something
in the cells says yes when our mouths say no—
the onward push, foot to the floor

of existence. An upward glance—
the typewriter key sticks again,
spitefully spoiling the ribbon.

The cells go on, so who is to blame
for this awful business of living.

II

Tearing up your photograph you feel
the distance between the grey-haired, cortisone-
heavy woman whose plumb face crumples

in your hand, and the woman who stuffs her
into the mouth of an over-spilling bin, begin
to disappear. Before, you laughed when people

seemed not to believe in a woman
who travelled alone, welcoming the solitude
of seeing nothing but the expanse of sea.

Smiling soberly, nobody heard the laughter
below, yourself breaking free like a fish flying
from the sea, momentarily disrupting the illusion

that what is hidden is the depth of the surface,
not the depth of what we cannot see.

III

Winter has culled the city, edging
all colour out. Salt covers ice, stark
and stubborn, on the pavements below.

You walk with your thoughts elsewhere, think
of the different worlds you have known.
There is little here to love—this is a place

where loneliness grows, where memories
wake you like a gun going off in the night
—a night that takes care of what you have done

or not done, of who you have loved
or not loved, of those you have saved,
or forgotten. You walk the winter streets,

hoping to catch the last of the light,
as it fades where the snow falls.

IV

The sun balloons in the sky, growing colder.
Through the window the air still feels
like summer—the water in the bay

still a blue that promises warmth,
though the sun that lights your room
is changing. Boston leaves hang on like flames

resisting extinction. Soon they will quell,
fall towards the earth, make themselves over.
Just as the body that sustains you gives way

to the carnival taking place inside
your brain—the inaudible crescendo
(or do you hear it?), that final giving in

when the blood vessel breaks—all life,
all memory too.

NOTES

PART I

'Graffiti on The Plant Store' refers to a specific piece of graffiti on the storefront of what used to be "The Plant Store" on Harcourt Street, Dublin. It consisted of the stencilled statement "You are beautiful".

'Nano's Dream Castle' is the title of Gerard Dillon's portrait of the artist Nano Reid.

The speaker in 'In Paint' is an imaginative rendering of Frida Kahlo.

'Eating Out' is indebted to Margaret Atwood's 'They Eat Out' from the collection *Power Politics*; also available in Margaret Atwood, *Eating Fire: Selected Poetry 1965-1995* (London: Virago Press, 2001).

PART II

The poems in Part II are inspired by the letters of Elizabeth Bishop. They are free and imaginative engagements with moments and perceptions—a turn of phrase, or fleeting observation—that inspired my thinking about Bishop while reading her letters, and remained in my mind thereafter. The resulting poems are an impressionistic response to passages in her letters that provided me with points of engagement, of reference, of departure—in short, inspiration—for this section.

'Accidents I' contains a partial quotation from Bishop's letter to Maria Osser, dated January 4, 1968: "but of course there is that business of 'going on living'—one does it, almost unconsciously—something in the cells, I think." The letter is to be found in *One Art: The Letters of Elizabeth Bishop*, selected and edited by Robert Giroux (New York: Farrar, Straus, and Giroux, 1994).